>>>———————————————————<<<

THIS BOOK BELONGS TO

>>>———————————————————<<<

A
B
C
D
E
F
G
H
I
J
K
L
M
N
O
P
Q
R
S
T
U
V
W
X
Y
Z

**WEBSITE**

EMAIL USED

USERNAME

PASSWORD

NOTES

**WEBSITE**

EMAIL USED

USERNAME

PASSWORD

NOTES

**WEBSITE**

EMAIL USED

USERNAME

PASSWORD

NOTES

## WEBSITE

EMAIL USED

USERNAME

PASSWORD

NOTES

## WEBSITE

EMAIL USED

USERNAME

PASSWORD

NOTES

## WEBSITE

EMAIL USED

USERNAME

PASSWORD

NOTES

A
B
C
D
E
F
G
H
I
J
K
L
M
N
O
P
Q
R
S
T
U
V
W
X
Y
Z

A

B

C | EMAIL USED

D | USERNAME

E
F | PASSWORD

G
H | NOTES

I

J | WEBSITE

K
L | EMAIL USED

M | USERNAME

N
O | PASSWORD

P
Q | NOTES

R

S | WEBSITE

T
U | EMAIL USED

V | USERNAME

W | PASSWORD
X

Y | NOTES
Z

## WEBSITE

EMAIL USED

USERNAME

PASSWORD

NOTES

## WEBSITE

EMAIL USED

USERNAME

PASSWORD

NOTES

## WEBSITE

EMAIL USED

USERNAME

PASSWORD

NOTES

A
B
C
D
E
F
G
H
I
J
K
L
M
N
O
P
Q
R
S
T
U
V
W
X
Y
Z

A
B
C — WEBSITE
D
E — EMAIL USED
F
G — USERNAME
H
I — PASSWORD
J
K — NOTES
L
M — WEBSITE
N
O — EMAIL USED
P
Q — USERNAME
R
S — PASSWORD
T
U — NOTES
V
W — WEBSITE
X
Y — EMAIL USED
Z — USERNAME

PASSWORD

NOTES

## WEBSITE

EMAIL USED

USERNAME

PASSWORD

NOTES

## WEBSITE

EMAIL USED

USERNAME

PASSWORD

NOTES

## WEBSITE

EMAIL USED

USERNAME

PASSWORD

NOTES

A
B
C
D
E
F
G
H
I
J
K
L
M
N
O
P
Q
R
S
T
U
V
W
X
Y
Z

A
B
C — WEBSITE

EMAIL USED

USERNAME

PASSWORD

NOTES

WEBSITE

EMAIL USED

USERNAME

PASSWORD

NOTES

WEBSITE

EMAIL USED

USERNAME

PASSWORD

NOTES

## WEBSITE

**EMAIL USED**

**USERNAME**

**PASSWORD**

**NOTES**

## WEBSITE

**EMAIL USED**

**USERNAME**

**PASSWORD**

**NOTES**

## WEBSITE

**EMAIL USED**

**USERNAME**

**PASSWORD**

**NOTES**

A
B
C
D
E
F
G
H
I
J
K
L
M
N
O
P
Q
R
S
T
U
V
W
X
Y
Z

A
B
C  WEBSITE

D  EMAIL USED

E  USERNAME

F  PASSWORD

G
H  NOTES

I
J  WEBSITE

K
L  EMAIL USED

M  USERNAME

N  PASSWORD
O

P  NOTES
Q

R
S  WEBSITE
T
U  EMAIL USED

V  USERNAME

W  PASSWORD
X

Y  NOTES
Z

## WEBSITE

**EMAIL USED**

**USERNAME**

**PASSWORD**

**NOTES**

## WEBSITE

**EMAIL USED**

**USERNAME**

**PASSWORD**

**NOTES**

## WEBSITE

**EMAIL USED**

**USERNAME**

**PASSWORD**

**NOTES**

A
B
C
D
E
F
G
H
I
J
K
L
M
N
O
P
Q
R
S
T
U
V
W
X
Y
Z

A
B
C  WEBSITE

D  EMAIL USED

E  USERNAME

F  PASSWORD

G
H  NOTES

I
J  WEBSITE

K
L  EMAIL USED

M  USERNAME

N  PASSWORD
O

P  NOTES
Q

R
S  WEBSITE

T
U  EMAIL USED

V  USERNAME

W  PASSWORD
X

Y  NOTES
Z

## WEBSITE

**EMAIL USED**

**USERNAME**

**PASSWORD**

**NOTES**

## WEBSITE

**EMAIL USED**

**USERNAME**

**PASSWORD**

**NOTES**

## WEBSITE

**EMAIL USED**

**USERNAME**

**PASSWORD**

**NOTES**

A
B
C
D
E
F
G
H
I
J
K
L
M
N
O
P
Q
R
S
T
U
V
W
X
Y
Z

A
B
| WEBSITE |

C
| EMAIL USED |

D
| USERNAME |

E
F
| PASSWORD |

G
H
| NOTES |

I
J
| WEBSITE |

K
L
| EMAIL USED |

M
| USERNAME |

N
O
| PASSWORD |

P
Q
| NOTES |

R
S
| WEBSITE |

T
U
| EMAIL USED |

V
| USERNAME |

W
| PASSWORD |

X
Y
| NOTES |

Z

## WEBSITE

EMAIL USED

USERNAME

PASSWORD

NOTES

## WEBSITE

EMAIL USED

USERNAME

PASSWORD

NOTES

## WEBSITE

EMAIL USED

USERNAME

PASSWORD

NOTES

A
B
C
**D**
E
F
G
H
I
J
K
L
M
N
O
P
Q
R
S
T
U
V
W
X
Y
Z

A
B
C
D
E
F
G
H
I
J
K
L
M
N
O
P
Q
R
S
T
U
V
W
X
Y
Z

**WEBSITE**

EMAIL USED

USERNAME

PASSWORD

NOTES

**WEBSITE**

EMAIL USED

USERNAME

PASSWORD

NOTES

**WEBSITE**

EMAIL USED

USERNAME

PASSWORD

NOTES

## WEBSITE

EMAIL USED

USERNAME

PASSWORD

NOTES

## WEBSITE

EMAIL USED

USERNAME

PASSWORD

NOTES

## WEBSITE

EMAIL USED

USERNAME

PASSWORD

NOTES

A
B
C
D
E
F
G
H
I
J
K
L
M
N
O
P
Q
R
S
T
U
V
W
X
Y
Z

WEBSITE

EMAIL USED

USERNAME

PASSWORD

NOTES

WEBSITE

EMAIL USED

USERNAME

PASSWORD

NOTES

WEBSITE

EMAIL USED

USERNAME

PASSWORD

NOTES

| WEBSITE |
|---|
| |

| EMAIL USED |
|---|
| |

| USERNAME |
|---|
| |

| PASSWORD |
|---|
| |

| NOTES |
|---|
| |

| WEBSITE |
|---|
| |

| EMAIL USED |
|---|
| |

| USERNAME |
|---|
| |

| PASSWORD |
|---|
| |

| NOTES |
|---|
| |

| WEBSITE |
|---|
| |

| EMAIL USED |
|---|
| |

| USERNAME |
|---|
| |

| PASSWORD |
|---|
| |

| NOTES |
|---|
| |

A B C D **E** F G H I J K L M N O P Q R S T U V W X Y Z

A
B
C
D
E
F
G
H
I
J
K
L
M
N
O
P
Q
R
S
T
U
V
W
X
Y
Z

WEBSITE

EMAIL USED

USERNAME

PASSWORD

NOTES

WEBSITE

EMAIL USED

USERNAME

PASSWORD

NOTES

WEBSITE

EMAIL USED

USERNAME

PASSWORD

NOTES

## WEBSITE

**EMAIL USED**

**USERNAME**

**PASSWORD**

**NOTES**

## WEBSITE

**EMAIL USED**

**USERNAME**

**PASSWORD**

**NOTES**

## WEBSITE

**EMAIL USED**

**USERNAME**

**PASSWORD**

**NOTES**

A
B
### WEBSITE

C
EMAIL USED

D
USERNAME

E
PASSWORD
F

G
NOTES
H

I
J
### WEBSITE

K
L
EMAIL USED

M
USERNAME

N
PASSWORD
O

P
NOTES
Q

R
S
### WEBSITE

T
U
EMAIL USED

V
USERNAME

W
PASSWORD
X

Y
NOTES
Z

## WEBSITE

**EMAIL USED**

**USERNAME**

**PASSWORD**

**NOTES**

## WEBSITE

**EMAIL USED**

**USERNAME**

**PASSWORD**

**NOTES**

## WEBSITE

**EMAIL USED**

**USERNAME**

**PASSWORD**

**NOTES**

A
B
WEBSITE

C  EMAIL USED

D  USERNAME

E
F  PASSWORD

G
H  NOTES

I
J  WEBSITE

K
L  EMAIL USED

M  USERNAME

N  PASSWORD

O

P  NOTES
Q

R
S  WEBSITE

T
U  EMAIL USED

V  USERNAME

W  PASSWORD
X

Y  NOTES
Z

| WEBSITE |
|---|
| |

| EMAIL USED |
|---|
| |

| USERNAME |
|---|
| |

| PASSWORD |
|---|
| |

| NOTES |
|---|
| |

| WEBSITE |
|---|
| |

| EMAIL USED |
|---|
| |

| USERNAME |
|---|
| |

| PASSWORD |
|---|
| |

| NOTES |
|---|
| |

| WEBSITE |
|---|
| |

| EMAIL USED |
|---|
| |

| USERNAME |
|---|
| |

| PASSWORD |
|---|
| |

| NOTES |
|---|
| |

A
B
C
D
E
**F**
G
H
I
J
K
L
M
N
O
P
Q
R
S
T
U
V
W
X
Y
Z

A
B
C
D
E
F
G
H
I
J
K
L
M
N
O
P
Q
R
S
T
U
V
W
X
Y
Z

WEBSITE

EMAIL USED

USERNAME

PASSWORD

NOTES

WEBSITE

EMAIL USED

USERNAME

PASSWORD

NOTES

WEBSITE

EMAIL USED

USERNAME

PASSWORD

NOTES

| WEBSITE |
|---|

| EMAIL USED |
|---|

| USERNAME |
|---|

| PASSWORD |
|---|

| NOTES |
|---|

| WEBSITE |
|---|

| EMAIL USED |
|---|

| USERNAME |
|---|

| PASSWORD |
|---|

| NOTES |
|---|

| WEBSITE |
|---|

| EMAIL USED |
|---|

| USERNAME |
|---|

| PASSWORD |
|---|

| NOTES |
|---|

A
B
C
D
E
F
G
H
I
J
K
L
M
N
O
P
Q
R
S
T
U
V
W
X
Y
Z

WEBSITE

EMAIL USED

USERNAME

PASSWORD

NOTES

WEBSITE

EMAIL USED

USERNAME

PASSWORD

NOTES

WEBSITE

EMAIL USED

USERNAME

PASSWORD

NOTES

**WEBSITE**

EMAIL USED

USERNAME

PASSWORD

NOTES

**WEBSITE**

EMAIL USED

USERNAME

PASSWORD

NOTES

**WEBSITE**

EMAIL USED

USERNAME

PASSWORD

NOTES

WEBSITE

EMAIL USED

USERNAME

PASSWORD

NOTES

WEBSITE

EMAIL USED

USERNAME

PASSWORD

NOTES

WEBSITE

EMAIL USED

USERNAME

PASSWORD

NOTES

| WEBSITE |
|---|

| EMAIL USED |
|---|

| USERNAME |
|---|

| PASSWORD |
|---|

| NOTES |
|---|

| WEBSITE |
|---|

| EMAIL USED |
|---|

| USERNAME |
|---|

| PASSWORD |
|---|

| NOTES |
|---|

| WEBSITE |
|---|

| EMAIL USED |
|---|

| USERNAME |
|---|

| PASSWORD |
|---|

| NOTES |
|---|

A B C D E F G **H** I J K L M N O P Q R S T U V W X Y Z

A
B
## WEBSITE

C
EMAIL USED

D
USERNAME

E
F
PASSWORD

G
H
NOTES

I
J
## WEBSITE

K
L
EMAIL USED

M
USERNAME

N
O
PASSWORD

P
Q
NOTES

R
S
## WEBSITE

T
U
EMAIL USED

V
USERNAME

W
X
PASSWORD

Y
Z
NOTES

| WEBSITE |
|---|

| EMAIL USED |
|---|

| USERNAME |
|---|

| PASSWORD |
|---|

| NOTES |
|---|

| WEBSITE |
|---|

| EMAIL USED |
|---|

| USERNAME |
|---|

| PASSWORD |
|---|

| NOTES |
|---|

| WEBSITE |
|---|

| EMAIL USED |
|---|

| USERNAME |
|---|

| PASSWORD |
|---|

| NOTES |
|---|

A
B
C
D
E
F
G
**H**
I
J
K
L
M
N
O
P
Q
R
S
T
U
V
W
X
Y
Z

A
B
| WEBSITE |

C | EMAIL USED |

D | USERNAME |

E
F | PASSWORD |

G
H | NOTES |

I

J
K | WEBSITE |

L | EMAIL USED |

M | USERNAME |

N
O | PASSWORD |

P
Q | NOTES |

R

S | WEBSITE |
T
U | EMAIL USED |

V | USERNAME |

W | PASSWORD |
X

Y | NOTES |
Z

| WEBSITE |
|---|

| EMAIL USED |
|---|

| USERNAME |
|---|

| PASSWORD |
|---|

| NOTES |
|---|

| WEBSITE |
|---|

| EMAIL USED |
|---|

| USERNAME |
|---|

| PASSWORD |
|---|

| NOTES |
|---|

| WEBSITE |
|---|

| EMAIL USED |
|---|

| USERNAME |
|---|

| PASSWORD |
|---|

| NOTES |
|---|

A
B
C | EMAIL USED
D | USERNAME
E
F | PASSWORD
G
H | NOTES
I
J | WEBSITE
K
L | EMAIL USED
M | USERNAME
N
O | PASSWORD
P
Q | NOTES
R
S | WEBSITE
T
U | EMAIL USED
V | USERNAME
W
X | PASSWORD
Y | NOTES
Z

**WEBSITE**

**EMAIL USED**

**USERNAME**

**PASSWORD**

**NOTES**

**WEBSITE**

**EMAIL USED**

**USERNAME**

**PASSWORD**

**NOTES**

**WEBSITE**

**EMAIL USED**

**USERNAME**

**PASSWORD**

**NOTES**

| WEBSITE |
|---|
|   |

| EMAIL USED |
|---|

| USERNAME |
|---|

| PASSWORD |
|---|
|   |

| NOTES |
|---|
|   |

| WEBSITE |
|---|
|   |

| EMAIL USED |
|---|

| USERNAME |
|---|

| PASSWORD |
|---|
|   |

| NOTES |
|---|
|   |

| WEBSITE |
|---|
|   |

| EMAIL USED |
|---|

| USERNAME |
|---|

| PASSWORD |
|---|
|   |

| NOTES |
|---|
|   |

A
B
C
D
E
F
G
H
I
J
K
L
M
N
O
P
Q
R
S
T
U
V
W
X
Y
Z

A
B
| WEBSITE |
|---|

C
| EMAIL USED |
|---|

D
| USERNAME |
|---|

E
F
| PASSWORD |
|---|

G
H
| NOTES |
|---|

I
J
| WEBSITE |
|---|

K
L
| EMAIL USED |
|---|

M
| USERNAME |
|---|

N
O
| PASSWORD |
|---|

P
Q
| NOTES |
|---|

R
S
| WEBSITE |
|---|

T
U
| EMAIL USED |
|---|

V
| USERNAME |
|---|

W
X
| PASSWORD |
|---|

Y
Z
| NOTES |
|---|

## WEBSITE

EMAIL USED

USERNAME

PASSWORD

NOTES

## WEBSITE

EMAIL USED

USERNAME

PASSWORD

NOTES

## WEBSITE

EMAIL USED

USERNAME

PASSWORD

NOTES

A
B
C
D
E
F
G
H
I
J
K
L
M
N
O
P
Q
R
S
T
U
V
W
X
Y
Z

A B C D E F G H I J K L M N O P Q R S T U V W X Y Z

WEBSITE

EMAIL USED

USERNAME

PASSWORD

NOTES

WEBSITE

EMAIL USED

USERNAME

PASSWORD

NOTES

WEBSITE

EMAIL USED

USERNAME

PASSWORD

NOTES

| WEBSITE | A |

EMAIL USED

USERNAME

PASSWORD

NOTES

| WEBSITE |

EMAIL USED

USERNAME

PASSWORD

NOTES

| WEBSITE |

EMAIL USED

USERNAME

PASSWORD

NOTES

A
B
C
D
E
F
G
H
I
J
K
L
M
N
O
P
Q
R
S
T
U
V
W
X
Y
Z

| | |
|---|---|
| A | **WEBSITE** |
| B | |
| C | EMAIL USED |
| D | USERNAME |
| E | PASSWORD |
| F | |
| G | NOTES |
| H | |
| I | |
| J | **WEBSITE** |
| K | |
| L | EMAIL USED |
| M | USERNAME |
| N | PASSWORD |
| O | |
| P | NOTES |
| Q | |
| R | |
| S | **WEBSITE** |
| T | |
| U | EMAIL USED |
| V | USERNAME |
| W | PASSWORD |
| X | |
| Y | NOTES |
| Z | |

WEBSITE

EMAIL USED

USERNAME

PASSWORD

NOTES

WEBSITE

EMAIL USED

USERNAME

PASSWORD

NOTES

WEBSITE

EMAIL USED

USERNAME

PASSWORD

NOTES

A
B
C
D
E
F
G
H
I
J
K
L
M
N
O
P
Q
R
S
T
U
V
W
X
Y
Z

A
B
C | EMAIL USED |
D | USERNAME |
E
F | PASSWORD |
G
H | NOTES |
I
J | WEBSITE |
K
L | EMAIL USED |
M | USERNAME |
N
O | PASSWORD |
P
Q | NOTES |
R
S | WEBSITE |
T
U | EMAIL USED |
V | USERNAME |
W
X | PASSWORD |
Y
Z | NOTES |

---

**WEBSITE**

| EMAIL USED |
| USERNAME |
| PASSWORD |
| NOTES |

**WEBSITE**

| EMAIL USED |
| USERNAME |
| PASSWORD |
| NOTES |

**WEBSITE**

| EMAIL USED |
| USERNAME |
| PASSWORD |
| NOTES |

## WEBSITE

EMAIL USED

USERNAME

PASSWORD

NOTES

## WEBSITE

EMAIL USED

USERNAME

PASSWORD

NOTES

## WEBSITE

EMAIL USED

USERNAME

PASSWORD

NOTES

A
B
C  EMAIL USED
D  USERNAME
E
F  PASSWORD
G
H  NOTES
I
J
K
L  EMAIL USED
M  USERNAME
N  PASSWORD
O
P  NOTES
Q
R
S
T
U  EMAIL USED
V  USERNAME
W  PASSWORD
X
Y  NOTES
Z

**WEBSITE**

**WEBSITE**

**WEBSITE**

## WEBSITE

**EMAIL USED**

**USERNAME**

**PASSWORD**

**NOTES**

## WEBSITE

**EMAIL USED**

**USERNAME**

**PASSWORD**

**NOTES**

## WEBSITE

**EMAIL USED**

**USERNAME**

**PASSWORD**

**NOTES**

| | WEBSITE |
|---|---|
| A | |
| B | |
| C | EMAIL USED |
| D | USERNAME |
| E | PASSWORD |
| F | |
| G | NOTES |
| H | |
| I | |
| J | WEBSITE |
| K | |
| L | EMAIL USED |
| M | USERNAME |
| N | PASSWORD |
| O | |
| P | NOTES |
| Q | |
| R | |
| S | WEBSITE |
| T | |
| U | EMAIL USED |
| V | USERNAME |
| W | PASSWORD |
| X | |
| Y | NOTES |
| Z | |

| WEBSITE |
|---|

| EMAIL USED |
|---|

| USERNAME |
|---|

| PASSWORD |
|---|

| NOTES |
|---|

| WEBSITE |
|---|

| EMAIL USED |
|---|

| USERNAME |
|---|

| PASSWORD |
|---|

| NOTES |
|---|

| WEBSITE |
|---|

| EMAIL USED |
|---|

| USERNAME |
|---|

| PASSWORD |
|---|

| NOTES |
|---|

A
B
C
D
E
F
G
H
I
J
K
**L**
M
N
O
P
Q
R
S
T
U
V
W
X
Y
Z

A
B
C   EMAIL USED
D   USERNAME
E
F   PASSWORD
G
H   NOTES
I
J                   WEBSITE
K
L   EMAIL USED
M   USERNAME
N   PASSWORD
O
P   NOTES
Q
R
S                   WEBSITE
T
U   EMAIL USED
V   USERNAME
W   PASSWORD
X
Y   NOTES
Z

## WEBSITE

**EMAIL USED**

**USERNAME**

**PASSWORD**

**NOTES**

## WEBSITE

**EMAIL USED**

**USERNAME**

**PASSWORD**

**NOTES**

## WEBSITE

**EMAIL USED**

**USERNAME**

**PASSWORD**

**NOTES**

A
B
C
D
E
F
G
H
I
J
K
L
**M**
N
O
P
Q
R
S
T
U
V
W
X
Y
Z

| | |
|---|---|
| A | **WEBSITE** |
| B | |
| C | EMAIL USED |
| D | USERNAME |
| E | |
| F | PASSWORD |
| G | |
| H | NOTES |
| I | |
| J | **WEBSITE** |
| K | |
| L | EMAIL USED |
| **M** | USERNAME |
| N | PASSWORD |
| O | |
| P | NOTES |
| Q | |
| R | |
| S | **WEBSITE** |
| T | |
| U | EMAIL USED |
| V | USERNAME |
| W | PASSWORD |
| X | |
| Y | NOTES |
| Z | |

## WEBSITE

EMAIL USED

USERNAME

PASSWORD

NOTES

## WEBSITE

EMAIL USED

USERNAME

PASSWORD

NOTES

## WEBSITE

EMAIL USED

USERNAME

PASSWORD

NOTES

| WEBSITE |
|---|
| |

| EMAIL USED |
|---|
| |

| USERNAME |
|---|
| |

| PASSWORD |
|---|
| |

| NOTES |
|---|
| |

| WEBSITE |
|---|
| |

| EMAIL USED |
|---|
| |

| USERNAME |
|---|
| |

| PASSWORD |
|---|
| |

| NOTES |
|---|
| |

| WEBSITE |
|---|
| |

| EMAIL USED |
|---|
| |

| USERNAME |
|---|
| |

| PASSWORD |
|---|
| |

| NOTES |
|---|
| |

| WEBSITE |
|---|
| |

| EMAIL USED |
|---|
| |

| USERNAME |
|---|
| |

| PASSWORD |
|---|
| |

| NOTES |
|---|
| |

| WEBSITE |
|---|
| |

| EMAIL USED |
|---|
| |

| USERNAME |
|---|
| |

| PASSWORD |
|---|
| |

| NOTES |
|---|
| |

| WEBSITE |
|---|
| |

| EMAIL USED |
|---|
| |

| USERNAME |
|---|
| |

| PASSWORD |
|---|
| |

| NOTES |
|---|
| |

A B C D E F G H I J K L M **N** O P Q R S T U V W X Y Z

A
B
| WEBSITE |

C  EMAIL USED

D  USERNAME

E
F  PASSWORD

G
H  NOTES

I
J
| WEBSITE |

K
L  EMAIL USED

M  USERNAME

N  PASSWORD
O

P
Q  NOTES

R
S
| WEBSITE |

T
U  EMAIL USED

V  USERNAME

W  PASSWORD
X

Y  NOTES
Z

**WEBSITE**

EMAIL USED

USERNAME

PASSWORD

NOTES

**WEBSITE**

EMAIL USED

USERNAME

PASSWORD

NOTES

**WEBSITE**

EMAIL USED

USERNAME

PASSWORD

NOTES

A
B
C
D
E
F
G
H
I
J
K
L
M
N
O
P
Q
R
S
T
U
V
W
X
Y
Z

A
B | **WEBSITE**
C | EMAIL USED
D | USERNAME
E
F | PASSWORD
G
H | NOTES
I
J | **WEBSITE**
K
L | EMAIL USED
M | USERNAME
N | PASSWORD
O
P
Q | NOTES
R
S | **WEBSITE**
T
U | EMAIL USED
V | USERNAME
W | PASSWORD
X
Y | NOTES
Z

| WEBSITE |
|---|

| EMAIL USED |
|---|

| USERNAME |
|---|

| PASSWORD |
|---|

| NOTES |
|---|

| WEBSITE |
|---|

| EMAIL USED |
|---|

| USERNAME |
|---|

| PASSWORD |
|---|

| NOTES |
|---|

| WEBSITE |
|---|

| EMAIL USED |
|---|

| USERNAME |
|---|

| PASSWORD |
|---|

| NOTES |
|---|

A B C D E F G H I J K L M N **O** P Q R S T U V W X Y Z

A
B
| WEBSITE |
|---|
| |

C
| EMAIL USED |
|---|
| |

D
| USERNAME |
|---|
| |

E
F
| PASSWORD |
|---|
| |

G
H
| NOTES |
|---|
| |

I
J
K
| WEBSITE |
|---|
| |

L
| EMAIL USED |
|---|
| |

M
| USERNAME |
|---|
| |

N
O
| PASSWORD |
|---|
| |

P
Q
| NOTES |
|---|
| |

R
S
T
| WEBSITE |
|---|
| |

U
| EMAIL USED |
|---|
| |

V
| USERNAME |
|---|
| |

W
X
| PASSWORD |
|---|
| |

Y
Z
| NOTES |
|---|
| |

| WEBSITE |
|---|

| EMAIL USED |
|---|

| USERNAME |
|---|

| PASSWORD |
|---|

| NOTES |
|---|

| WEBSITE |
|---|

| EMAIL USED |
|---|

| USERNAME |
|---|

| PASSWORD |
|---|

| NOTES |
|---|

| WEBSITE |
|---|

| EMAIL USED |
|---|

| USERNAME |
|---|

| PASSWORD |
|---|

| NOTES |
|---|

A
B
C
D
E
F
G
H
I
J
K
L
M
N
**O**
P
Q
R
S
T
U
V
W
X
Y
Z

A
B
| WEBSITE |

C  EMAIL USED

D  USERNAME

E
F  PASSWORD

G
H  NOTES

I
J
| WEBSITE |

K
L  EMAIL USED

M  USERNAME

N  PASSWORD

O
P  NOTES
Q

R
S
| WEBSITE |

T
U  EMAIL USED

V  USERNAME

W  PASSWORD
X

Y  NOTES
Z

## WEBSITE

EMAIL USED

USERNAME

PASSWORD

NOTES

## WEBSITE

EMAIL USED

USERNAME

PASSWORD

NOTES

## WEBSITE

EMAIL USED

USERNAME

PASSWORD

NOTES

A
B
C
D
E
F
G
H
I
J
K
L
M
N
O
P
Q
R
S
T
U
V
W
X
Y
Z

WEBSITE

EMAIL USED

USERNAME

PASSWORD

NOTES

WEBSITE

EMAIL USED

USERNAME

PASSWORD

NOTES

WEBSITE

EMAIL USED

USERNAME

PASSWORD

NOTES

## WEBSITE

EMAIL USED

USERNAME

PASSWORD

NOTES

## WEBSITE

EMAIL USED

USERNAME

PASSWORD

NOTES

## WEBSITE

EMAIL USED

USERNAME

PASSWORD

NOTES

A
B
| WEBSITE |

C  EMAIL USED

D  USERNAME

E
F  PASSWORD

G
H  NOTES

I
J
| WEBSITE |

K
L  EMAIL USED

M  USERNAME

N
O  PASSWORD

P
Q  NOTES

R
S
| WEBSITE |

T
U  EMAIL USED

V  USERNAME

W  PASSWORD
X

Y  NOTES
Z

| WEBSITE |

| EMAIL USED |

| USERNAME |

| PASSWORD |

| NOTES |

| WEBSITE |

| EMAIL USED |

| USERNAME |

| PASSWORD |

| NOTES |

| WEBSITE |

| EMAIL USED |

| USERNAME |

| PASSWORD |

| NOTES |

A
B
C
D
E
F
G
H
I
J
K
L
M
N
O
P
Q
R
S
T
U
V
W
X
Y
Z

A
B
| WEBSITE |

C
| EMAIL USED |

D
| USERNAME |

E
F
| PASSWORD |

G
H
| NOTES |

I
J
| WEBSITE |

K
L
| EMAIL USED |

M
| USERNAME |

N
O
| PASSWORD |

P
Q
| NOTES |

R
S
| WEBSITE |

T
U
| EMAIL USED |

V
| USERNAME |

W
X
| PASSWORD |

Y
Z
| NOTES |

## WEBSITE

EMAIL USED

USERNAME

PASSWORD

NOTES

## WEBSITE

EMAIL USED

USERNAME

PASSWORD

NOTES

## WEBSITE

EMAIL USED

USERNAME

PASSWORD

NOTES

## R

**WEBSITE**

EMAIL USED

USERNAME

PASSWORD

NOTES

**WEBSITE**

EMAIL USED

USERNAME

PASSWORD

NOTES

**WEBSITE**

EMAIL USED

USERNAME

PASSWORD

NOTES

## WEBSITE

**EMAIL USED**

**USERNAME**

**PASSWORD**

**NOTES**

## WEBSITE

**EMAIL USED**

**USERNAME**

**PASSWORD**

**NOTES**

## WEBSITE

**EMAIL USED**

**USERNAME**

**PASSWORD**

**NOTES**

A
B
C
D
E
F
G
H
I
J
K
L
M
N
O
P
Q
**R**
S
T
U
V
W
X
Y
Z

A
B          WEBSITE

C    EMAIL USED

D    USERNAME

E
F    PASSWORD

G
H    NOTES

I
J          WEBSITE
K
L    EMAIL USED

M    USERNAME

N    PASSWORD
O

P    NOTES
Q

R
S          WEBSITE
T
U    EMAIL USED

V    USERNAME

W    PASSWORD
X

Y    NOTES
Z

| WEBSITE |
|---|

| EMAIL USED |
|---|

| USERNAME |
|---|

| PASSWORD |
|---|

| NOTES |
|---|

| WEBSITE |
|---|

| EMAIL USED |
|---|

| USERNAME |
|---|

| PASSWORD |
|---|

| NOTES |
|---|

| WEBSITE |
|---|

| EMAIL USED |
|---|

| USERNAME |
|---|

| PASSWORD |
|---|

| NOTES |
|---|

A B C D E F G H I J K L M N O P Q **R** S T U V W X Y Z

A
B
## WEBSITE

C    EMAIL USED

D    USERNAME

E
F    PASSWORD

G
H    NOTES

I
J
## WEBSITE

K
L    EMAIL USED

M    USERNAME

N    PASSWORD
O

P    NOTES
Q

R
S
## WEBSITE

T
U    EMAIL USED

V    USERNAME

W    PASSWORD
X

Y    NOTES
Z

## WEBSITE

EMAIL USED

USERNAME

PASSWORD

NOTES

## WEBSITE

EMAIL USED

USERNAME

PASSWORD

NOTES

## WEBSITE

EMAIL USED

USERNAME

PASSWORD

NOTES

A
B
C
D
E
F
G
H
I
J
K
L
M
N
O
P
Q
R
**S**
T
U
V
W
X
Y
Z

A
B
C  WEBSITE

D  EMAIL USED

E
F  USERNAME

G  PASSWORD

H
I  NOTES

J  WEBSITE

K
L  EMAIL USED

M  USERNAME

N  PASSWORD

O

P  NOTES

Q
R

S  WEBSITE

T
U  EMAIL USED

V  USERNAME

W  PASSWORD

X
Y  NOTES

Z

## WEBSITE

**EMAIL USED**

**USERNAME**

**PASSWORD**

**NOTES**

## WEBSITE

**EMAIL USED**

**USERNAME**

**PASSWORD**

**NOTES**

## WEBSITE

**EMAIL USED**

**USERNAME**

**PASSWORD**

**NOTES**

A B C D E F G H I J K L M N O P Q R **S** T U V W X Y Z

A
B
| WEBSITE |

C | EMAIL USED |

D | USERNAME |

E
F | PASSWORD |

G
H | NOTES |

I
J
| WEBSITE |

K
L | EMAIL USED |

M | USERNAME |

N
O | PASSWORD |

P
Q | NOTES |

R
S
| WEBSITE |

T
U | EMAIL USED |

V | USERNAME |

W
X | PASSWORD |

Y
Z | NOTES |

## WEBSITE

EMAIL USED

USERNAME

PASSWORD

NOTES

## WEBSITE

EMAIL USED

USERNAME

PASSWORD

NOTES

## WEBSITE

EMAIL USED

USERNAME

PASSWORD

NOTES

A
B
## WEBSITE

C   EMAIL USED

D   USERNAME

E
F   PASSWORD

G
H   NOTES

I
J
## WEBSITE

K
L   EMAIL USED

M   USERNAME

N   PASSWORD
O

P   NOTES
Q

R
S
## WEBSITE

T
U   EMAIL USED

V   USERNAME

W   PASSWORD
X

Y   NOTES
Z

## WEBSITE

EMAIL USED

USERNAME

PASSWORD

NOTES

## WEBSITE

EMAIL USED

USERNAME

PASSWORD

NOTES

## WEBSITE

EMAIL USED

USERNAME

PASSWORD

NOTES

A
B
C
D
E
F
G
H
I
J
K
L
M
N
O
P
Q
R
S
T
U
V
W
X
Y
Z

| | WEBSITE |
|---|---|
| A | |
| B | |
| C | EMAIL USED |
| D | USERNAME |
| E | |
| F | PASSWORD |
| G | |
| H | NOTES |
| I | |

| | WEBSITE |
|---|---|
| J | |
| K | |
| L | EMAIL USED |
| M | USERNAME |
| N | PASSWORD |
| O | |
| P | NOTES |
| Q | |
| R | |

| | WEBSITE |
|---|---|
| S | |
| T | |
| U | EMAIL USED |
| V | USERNAME |
| W | PASSWORD |
| X | |
| Y | NOTES |
| Z | |

| WEBSITE |

| EMAIL USED |

| USERNAME |

| PASSWORD |

| NOTES |

| WEBSITE |

| EMAIL USED |

| USERNAME |

| PASSWORD |

| NOTES |

| WEBSITE |

| EMAIL USED |

| USERNAME |

| PASSWORD |

| NOTES |

A
B
C
D
E
F
G
H
I
J
K
L
M
N
O
P
Q
R
S
T
U
V
W
X
Y
Z

A
B
## WEBSITE

C
EMAIL USED

D
USERNAME

E
PASSWORD
F

G
NOTES
H

I

J
## WEBSITE

K
EMAIL USED
L

M
USERNAME

N
PASSWORD
O

P
NOTES
Q

R

S
## WEBSITE

T
EMAIL USED
U

V
USERNAME

W
PASSWORD
X

Y
NOTES
Z

## WEBSITE

EMAIL USED

USERNAME

PASSWORD

NOTES

## WEBSITE

EMAIL USED

USERNAME

PASSWORD

NOTES

## WEBSITE

EMAIL USED

USERNAME

PASSWORD

NOTES

A
B
## WEBSITE

C   EMAIL USED

D   USERNAME

E
F   PASSWORD

G
H   NOTES

I
J
## WEBSITE

K
L   EMAIL USED

M   USERNAME

N   PASSWORD
O

P   NOTES
Q

R
S
## WEBSITE

T
U   EMAIL USED

V   USERNAME

W   PASSWORD
X

Y   NOTES
Z

| WEBSITE |
|---|
| EMAIL USED |
| USERNAME |
| PASSWORD |
| NOTES |

| WEBSITE |
|---|
| EMAIL USED |
| USERNAME |
| PASSWORD |
| NOTES |

| WEBSITE |
|---|
| EMAIL USED |
| USERNAME |
| PASSWORD |
| NOTES |

A B C D E F G H I J K L M N O P Q R S T U **V** W X Y Z

A
B
| WEBSITE |
|---|
| |

C | EMAIL USED |
|---|

D | USERNAME |
|---|

E
F
| PASSWORD |
|---|
| |

G
H
| NOTES |
|---|
| |

I
J
| WEBSITE |
|---|
| |

K
L
| EMAIL USED |
|---|

M | USERNAME |
|---|

N
O
| PASSWORD |
|---|
| |

P
Q
| NOTES |
|---|
| |

R
S
| WEBSITE |
|---|
| |

T
U
| EMAIL USED |
|---|

V | USERNAME |
|---|

W
X
| PASSWORD |
|---|
| |

Y
Z
| NOTES |
|---|
| |

| WEBSITE |

| EMAIL USED |

| USERNAME |

| PASSWORD |

| NOTES |

| WEBSITE |

| EMAIL USED |

| USERNAME |

| PASSWORD |

| NOTES |

| WEBSITE |

| EMAIL USED |

| USERNAME |

| PASSWORD |

| NOTES |

A
B
| WEBSITE |
|---|
| |

C
| EMAIL USED |
|---|
| |

D
| USERNAME |
|---|
| |

E
F
| PASSWORD |
|---|
| |

G
| NOTES |
|---|
| |
H

I
J
| WEBSITE |
|---|
| |

K
L
| EMAIL USED |
|---|
| |

M
| USERNAME |
|---|
| |

N
| PASSWORD |
|---|
| |
O

P
| NOTES |
|---|
| |
Q

R
S
| WEBSITE |
|---|
| |

T
U
| EMAIL USED |
|---|
| |

V
| USERNAME |
|---|
| |

W
| PASSWORD |
|---|
| |
X

Y
| NOTES |
|---|
| |
Z

## WEBSITE

EMAIL USED

USERNAME

PASSWORD

NOTES

## WEBSITE

EMAIL USED

USERNAME

PASSWORD

NOTES

## WEBSITE

EMAIL USED

USERNAME

PASSWORD

NOTES

A
B
| WEBSITE |

C  EMAIL USED

D  USERNAME

E
F  PASSWORD

G
H  NOTES

I
J
| WEBSITE |

K
L  EMAIL USED

M  USERNAME

N  PASSWORD
O

P  NOTES
Q

R
S
| WEBSITE |

T
U  EMAIL USED

V  USERNAME

W  PASSWORD
X

Y  NOTES
Z

## WEBSITE

EMAIL USED

USERNAME

PASSWORD

NOTES

## WEBSITE

EMAIL USED

USERNAME

PASSWORD

NOTES

## WEBSITE

EMAIL USED

USERNAME

PASSWORD

NOTES

| WEBSITE |
|---|
| |

| EMAIL USED |
|---|
| |

| USERNAME |
|---|
| |

| PASSWORD |
|---|
| |

| NOTES |
|---|
| |

| WEBSITE |
|---|
| |

| EMAIL USED |
|---|
| |

| USERNAME |
|---|
| |

| PASSWORD |
|---|
| |

| NOTES |
|---|
| |

| WEBSITE |
|---|
| |

| EMAIL USED |
|---|
| |

| USERNAME |
|---|
| |

| PASSWORD |
|---|
| |

| NOTES |
|---|
| |

| WEBSITE |
|---|

| EMAIL USED |
|---|

| USERNAME |
|---|

| PASSWORD |
|---|

| NOTES |
|---|

| WEBSITE |
|---|

| EMAIL USED |
|---|

| USERNAME |
|---|

| PASSWORD |
|---|

| NOTES |
|---|

| WEBSITE |
|---|

| EMAIL USED |
|---|

| USERNAME |
|---|

| PASSWORD |
|---|

| NOTES |
|---|

A
B
WEBSITE

C EMAIL USED

D USERNAME

E
PASSWORD
F

G
NOTES
H

I

J WEBSITE

K
L EMAIL USED

M USERNAME

N
PASSWORD
O

P
NOTES
Q

R

S WEBSITE

T
U EMAIL USED

V USERNAME

W PASSWORD
X

Y NOTES
Z

## WEBSITE

EMAIL USED

USERNAME

PASSWORD

NOTES

## WEBSITE

EMAIL USED

USERNAME

PASSWORD

NOTES

## WEBSITE

EMAIL USED

USERNAME

PASSWORD

NOTES

A
B
C
D
E
F
G
H
I
J
K
L
M
N
O
P
Q
R
S
T
U
V
W
X
Y
Z

A
B
| WEBSITE |
|---|
| |

C | EMAIL USED |
D | USERNAME |
E
F | PASSWORD |
G
H | NOTES |
I

J
K
| WEBSITE |
|---|
| |

L | EMAIL USED |
M | USERNAME |
N
O | PASSWORD |
P
Q | NOTES |
R

S
T
| WEBSITE |
|---|
| |

U | EMAIL USED |
V | USERNAME |
W
X | PASSWORD |
Y
Z | NOTES |

## WEBSITE

**EMAIL USED**

**USERNAME**

**PASSWORD**

**NOTES**

## WEBSITE

**EMAIL USED**

**USERNAME**

**PASSWORD**

**NOTES**

## WEBSITE

**EMAIL USED**

**USERNAME**

**PASSWORD**

**NOTES**

A
B | **WEBSITE**
C | EMAIL USED
D | USERNAME
E
F | PASSWORD
G
H | NOTES
I
J | **WEBSITE**
K
L | EMAIL USED
M | USERNAME
N | PASSWORD
O
P | NOTES
Q
R
S | **WEBSITE**
T
U | EMAIL USED
V | USERNAME
W | PASSWORD
X
Y | NOTES
Z

| WEBSITE |

| EMAIL USED |
| USERNAME |
| PASSWORD |

| NOTES |

| WEBSITE |

| EMAIL USED |
| USERNAME |
| PASSWORD |

| NOTES |

| WEBSITE |

| EMAIL USED |
| USERNAME |
| PASSWORD |

| NOTES |

A
B
## WEBSITE

C EMAIL USED

D USERNAME

E
F PASSWORD

G
H NOTES

I

J
## WEBSITE

K
L EMAIL USED

M USERNAME

N PASSWORD
O

P
Q NOTES

R

S
## WEBSITE

T
U EMAIL USED

V USERNAME

W PASSWORD
X

Y NOTES
Z

## WEBSITE

EMAIL USED

USERNAME

PASSWORD

NOTES

## WEBSITE

EMAIL USED

USERNAME

PASSWORD

NOTES

## WEBSITE

EMAIL USED

USERNAME

PASSWORD

NOTES

A
B | WEBSITE
C | EMAIL USED
D | USERNAME
E
F | PASSWORD
G
H | NOTES
I
J | WEBSITE
K
L | EMAIL USED
M | USERNAME
N | PASSWORD
O
P | NOTES
Q
R
S | WEBSITE
T
U | EMAIL USED
V | USERNAME
W | PASSWORD
X
Y | NOTES
Z

## WEBSITE

**EMAIL USED**

**USERNAME**

**PASSWORD**

**NOTES**

## WEBSITE

**EMAIL USED**

**USERNAME**

**PASSWORD**

**NOTES**

## WEBSITE

**EMAIL USED**

**USERNAME**

**PASSWORD**

**NOTES**

# NOTES

# NOTES

# NOTES

# NOTES

Copyright © 2019
All rights reserved. No part of this publication may be reproduced, distributed,
or transmitted in any form or by any means, including photocopying, recording,
or other electronic or mechanical methods, without the prior written permission
of the publisher, except in the case of brief quotations embodied in critical reviews
and certain other noncommercial uses permitted by copyright law.

www.ingramcontent.com/pod-product-compliance
Lightning Source LLC
Chambersburg PA
CBHW070420220526
45466CB00004B/1476